For Si & Diana,

With many thanks
for your friendship.

2/14/78

Of Sons and Seasons

William S. Cohen

Simon and Schuster
New York

Drawings by Ron Hyams

Designed by Irving Perkins
Manufactured in the United States of America
1 2 3 4 5 6 7 8 9 10

Library of Congress Cataloging in Publication Data

Cohen, William S
    Of sons and seasons.

    I. Title.
PS3553.043403   811'.5'4   77-18758
ISBN 0-671-24054-4

To Clara and Ruby Cohen
and to Diane, Kevin and Chris,
with enduring gratitude

Contents

Foreword

THE USES of poetry—the reasons for writing it—have been the subjects of debate at least since Athens went to political rot and philosophic glory. Aristotle thought of poetry as a secondary device for discerning reality, the Elizabethans used it as an expository avenue to two separate realities—the world of the external senses and the internal world known through intuition. Shelley said that poets were the legislators of mankind, Eliot thought of the poem as a sort of newspaper column reporting—or speculating upon—transcendent events in human life. Robert Lowell used it to shred his own life and experience down to the true and often excruciating bone.

All of this discussion has, until lately, ignored the question of who should write poetry. Poetry began as popular entertainment. Homer and the great authors of the Nordic oral tradition meant their stuff to be chanted in smoky halls and marketplaces. Shakespeare wrote drama for popular audiences. Somewhere along the line—it was sometime in the late eighteenth or early nineteenth century, I suppose—poetry got overwhelmed by more accessible amusements and instructions. The art was relegated to slender volumes read by A Very Few People. Poets turned professional; they were issued implicit licenses to practice by critics, publishers and the people who read them. It's interesting to speculate on how Sophocles would have been recieved in the present poetic climate.

9

He was a rich man who spent most of his time as a general, priest and politician; his 120-odd poetic dramas were the works of an amateur competing for prizes during religious festivals.

The author of the poems which follow is many things. He is a member of the United States Congress, a leading figure in the moderate wing of the Republican party, a scholar, superb athlete, jazz buff, occasional contributor of political articles to newspapers, reader, speculator on the nature of things.

The multiplicity of Bill Cohen's life doesn't disqualify him as a poet simply because poetry is only one of the many things that he does well. Indeed, that very multiplicity of Bill's life is the source of his poems. The immense diversity of subject matter in this book of verses is one of its principal fascinations. Many poets have extracted the alchemy of love and death from the marrow of their being. None that I know of has written about impeachment, the dank stench of personal political corruption or the experiences of a prosecuting attorney.

Bill Cohen is part of an older poetic setting. He is a poet who writes true occasional verse that is derived from a life lived at the center of contemporary public affairs. He writes for the same reason that all genuine poets do— because *not* writing is unbearable; life cannot be contained without expressing it.

The question is not who *should* write poetry. It is a question of who *must*. Bill Cohen must because he carries within him what the American novelist Charles McCarry once called "the indispensible wound"—that surface of sensibility scraped raw and vulnerable to intuitive as well as intellectual perception.

To describe the Congressman-poet as a man would be to violate the intention of the poems in his book. His self-portrait follows. As his friend and reader I can only attest to its accuracy.

That and one thing more: some years ago during some public uproar or other I wrote in a newspaper column that "the politics of poets shouldn't be taken any more seriously than the poetry of politicians." Having read Bill Cohen's poetry, any humiliation I might feel in conceding that I was wrong in saying that is more than offset by the pleasure given me by the work of this poet who is also a politician.

Rod MacLeish

Washington, 1977

I wish to express my deep appreciation to Ed and Sheila Weidenfeld for their encouragement, assistance and counsel in helping to make this book possible.

My special thanks to my editors, Nan Talese and Jonathan Coleman, for the many hours they spent with me on the manuscript.

Of Sons and Seasons

Introduction

A POEM is a window into the soul of the writer. A collection of poems, in a way, is biography—a travelogue that reveals the route of a personal journey. But it is biography without the baggage of historical explanation, anecdote or embellishment.

If the words are finely tuned and acoustically arranged, then they will fall upon the inner ear without the need of accompaniment; if they are not, then a full orchestration, with bass and brass, will not transmute their cacophony.

To be mindful of the folly of attempting to explain or add to a given poem is not to suggest that one can resist the temptation. Friends have suggested that I am a very public man and my poems private experiences, that it would be interesting to reveal the circumstances under which they were written. The politician in me emerges and suggests a compromise. If it will help in some instances to wipe the window a little cleaner with more words, then I shall do so. But I do so with the knowledge that exposition that seeks to remove obscurity runs the risk of explaining too much, and destroying the allure of ambiguity.

The Poet

He fights
the hour with ink,
struggling to lift his words
beyond their brief cry,
before the vision in his eye
fades and dissipates
in its bone vault.

He labors
to construct with the
backbone of his tongue,
a cursive monument
that will endure
like Big Sur sea cliffs
against the sun,
against the wind
and all oblivion.

He writes
poems with his fretful pen,
hoping but one rhyme
will survive and fossilize
in the long thought of Time.

Part One

I was born August 28, 1940, in a three-story apartment house in Bangor, Maine. The second of three children, all born in our mother's bed—whether out of economy or general fear of hospitals, I don't know. Hancock Street was one of the poorer sections of the city. It was filled with families from the "old country." There were several beer parlors and bootleggers in the neighborhood. Morris Slep's meat market was next door (the image of Mr. Slep's bloody apron and quick and precise hands is still vivid in my mind). The Pyzynski family had a store across the street. Mrs. Soloby owned the apartment building where we lived. My Aunt Gertrude (Gittle) and my grandfather, an immigrant from Russia, lived in one of the apartments on the second floor. In the attic above us, Mrs. Soloby provided cots for harmless old men who had no place to sleep. They always came up the back stairs and so I rarely saw them. But I always remember the sound of their footsteps over our bedroom, as they shuffled back and forth during the nights.

Hancock Street was a microcosm of a part of life that could be found in any city, in any country. People locked into a life cycle of struggle and survival, who rarely escaped. It was a street littered with men who had failed, never got started, who sat on doorsteps and let the sun sink into their haggard faces flushed red with wine and filled with veins that had broken and spread wide from the alcohol that they strained from canned heat through soiled handkerchiefs.

They would sit and watch cars pass them by, heads swimming in confusion, unaware of or indifferent to the looks of contempt flashed by occupants of the fleeting vehicles.

I spent the first seven years of my life on that street. And while my mother kept me under her watchful and protective eye most of the time, it was not an ideal place in which to grow up. It was a tough neighborhood, and you had to demonstrate that you were tough, too, or you became the repeated victim of the other kids' aggression. Silly as it seems to me now, I recall that between the ages of five and seven, I spent a good deal of time fighting, trying to establish a reputation as someone not to mess with.

Even after we moved from Hancock Street, I continued to go back. My father's bakery was just a few blocks from the apartment house, and I worked at the bakery part-time until I graduated from high school.

But even when I wasn't working at the bakery, I used to drive up the street, looking into the faces of my former friends and enemies. I was no longer one of them, but I never wanted to forget that I once had been.

All of that part of my past is gone now. Sammy's Barber Shop, Caruso's Spaghetti House, Gotlieb's Meat Market, the bars with their garish lights—all have been swept away in the name of urban renewal.

Hancock Street is now only a memory for me, an important one that I hope will not fade as the years accumulate. It was not just a street. It was a place, a condition that has always been and one that we can only hope will not always be.

Hancock Street

It's gone.
The place where
I was born.

So many years
it stood tall and brown
on that street of immigrants
who spoke in broken accents
and unshattered hopes.

The memory of
the butcher next door
with red fingers
and quick hands;
the barber who
clipped my yellow hair
with lyrical scissors
that sang of Italy.
And those unshaven lost
who slept on steps and
in vacant lots
reeking of wine and canned heat
squeezed into handkerchiefs,
reeling, red-faced,
demeaned and demeaning . . .

I returned over the years,
unashamed, to that street
to reaffirm my roots,
my birth, my beginning,
to test the strength
of the line strung
from my past, knowing
after all my wanderings
I should be buried
on a hill not far
from that house
to complete the triangle
of my destiny.

But the points of reference
have been withdrawn
under some urban
planner's strategy
to replace the rot
with a new vitality
and wipe away
all memory and myth
of Hancock Street's history.

Birth House. Perhaps you knew
that like other buildings
on the block,
you were destined
to be picked apart,
floor by floor,
board by board,
the flesh of your carcass
ripped, a giant brown fish,
by a score of minnows
quickened with courage
by their numbers
and your decay.

Perhaps that's why
you tried suicide,
a flash fire of unknown origin
just days before demolition
was scheduled to begin.

At least by igniting
and sending flames and ashes
showering into the night,
that might be some
final and fitting testament
to the life that you had known,
the cries of birth and death
that stained your walls
and etched your soul
with joy and pain.

But you met
with only half success.
Rescue came too soon
and left you standing,
scorched black and windowless.

You are gone now, finally.
The cranes and trucks
came and carted you off
in pieces.

The signs still read
Hancock Street, Bangor, Maine,
but it's not the same.

And I find myself
singing verses, stringing lyrical
lines in a larger void,

searching for some new hill
to mark my name.

Larger Now
In Memory of Andrew S. Pennell

Time ticked slow
for me when I was young,
it took so long to grow
("Come measure me,
will I be tall as a tree?")
until that moment
in reaching to outreach
my father, I found him old.

I am larger, Father, taller,
but you seem to grow smaller
each day, as if nature,
once engaged in play,
suddenly turned
to complete her course
and take you back
to an aged infancy.

The wheel of time
weighs like a stone
upon your back,
the signs are in your eyes
but how you do pretend
that age knows no circumference!
Infinity will one day add your dust
to its boundless bin,
but how you do contend
with a wink and grin
that you will always
catch each dawn
breaking through the window
of your work.

That moment will come
when the night will shake
with our mother's cries,
tears will fill her eyes,
but you will be gone,
beyond prayers or promises.

Father, I would join
you now in eternity
but my sons still
look to outreach me;
I cannot fall,
not until they are tall
and I am small
and the cycle
complete.

One day we may again
share the same horizon,
perhaps conscious, perhaps not,
but knowing now the sun
was ours once then.

And with the blade
of having been,
took reluctant leave
from our shrinking selves,
carving a mark
into the bark
of an ancient tree.

Part Two

WASHINGTON IS essentially a city of transients, new faces moving in and out, new Presidents, Congressmen, Cabinet officers, foreign service diplomats—the unrelenting flow of the Potomac. And with each wave of new faces, a certain hope flickers in all but the most hardened hearts of Washington-based journalists and news commentators that life somehow will be better, the economy will improve, the national malaise will evaporate. It is the belief that the world is still malleable and our country can be squeezed and reshaped to fit its former greatness and once again glow in a gilded era of history. It is the same optimism that each spring brings, the sensuous feeling of dull roots stirring under the layers of cold earth, of brittle branches leaking green leaves to flutter in the currents of warm wind.

Inauguration Day is always a special moment in Washington. January 20, 1977, was even more so. A man from the Deep South, virtually unknown just a year before, was about to take the oath of the highest office in the land.

In a year filled with countless interviews, personal profiles and human interest stories, journalists had tried to inform the public of the character of their potential new leader, and, if possible, to discover the blueprint of his personality so that his future actions could be predicted or prevented.

The American people expected change. Not knowing what kind of change we wanted or what kind we would receive only added to the drama of the day.

Inauguration Day, 1977

Ice and cold
cut into the marrow
of bones,
brittle but bright
with Georgian smiles.

Electronic eyes swept
across the nation's marbled steps
laminating on film
history's curious need
for the deed of power
deposed and transferred.

Trumpets blared, drums beat,
throngs were brought
to their feet
as southern voices sang
northern battle hymns.

In just a moment
greatness flickered
and fell as the sun's
shadow crossed noon.

The President's mantle
was draped then,
on smaller shoulders,
a softer voice spoke,
with a preacher's
cadence and lilt.

A promise of less,
a plea for more
kindness, charity,
        commitment, humility,
laughter and, yes, family.

Let us spread our promise
of peace not with
the weapons of war
through the eye of madness,
but, if we can, as gentle
and sure as a flower unfolding
its petals to the sun.

Even in the whiteness
of winter's arctic breath,
among the mufflers, gloves
and overcoats,
the color of green,
the spirit of bloom
seemed to stir
in the barren trees.

It was cold.
The people were warm enough
inside with the dusted off
dreams of
America.

Second-Story Book Store

Pages pressed between
water-soaked and warped
boards of cloth.

Hieroglyphics heaped
in deep layers of ink,
indecipherable in their mass.

Strangers come here picking
through faded titles,
sifting through the rubble
in search of a fragment,
some clue to the fate
of an ancient state
that rose and fell
under the weight
of crumbling time.

As if the words
could turn to keys
and unlock the
rusty rehearsal
of old mistakes
that we repeat
on the future's
shrinking stage.

I hold this volume.
I swing my axe,
hoping it will strike
some secret stone.

Memorial Day

For Tom and Elizabeth Lambert

Memorial Day is a moment
when celebration and sadness
are joined hand in hand
in a strident brass band march
on every Main Street
at 10 A.M.

It is a holiday weekend
filled with pain
and potted flowers
for some,
you know the ones,
who circle through manicured lawns
in a quiet drone,
searching for those now gone
sunk in brevity,
carved in stone.

A time for families
to gather from distant coasts
and drop tears over the memory
of tall ghosts,
sons or brothers
who gave their green for all
and forever.

Then there is the parade
where balloons and miniature flags
are held by babies
resting on their fathers' height
and the shirt-sleeved crowd
rejoices at the sight
of some friend who steps left
when the sergeant barks right.

A veteran from some ancient war
steps proudly to a patriotic beat and blare,
his frozen face, the subject once
of an artist's special grace,
strapped in a metal disc
that gave thin shelter
against the risk
of destruction.

By the reviewing stand
pass ROTC units, then
a local high school band,
and there, in the very rear,
dressed in blue shirts and bright scarves,
comes the smallest group,
the youngest troop.
Cub scouts, with
blushing flower faces
and embarrassed grins,
unsure of their presence,
of their particular
significance.

Is it simply the promise
of a continuing nation
or is it instead
a subtler solace to those
who mourn their dead,
that these sons of others
will one day answer
a written call
and stand ready to fall
in some foreign land
in the name of freedom?

I really don't know,
I only ask because today
my son was somewhere
in that parade
and I couldn't bear to
go.

Song of Song My

The morning headlines and evening news
Picked a sheet of music
From the repertoire of war
And scanned the meter of madness,
Singing us the melody
Of guns and gore:

In the village of Song My
Walked G.I. Joe
Searching for the Foe
Looking for the Foe, Joe.

Slat-thin people
And small children
Were strung between the chorus
Of defining the enemy:

"You helped the V.C."
"But against our Will."
"No matter, you gave them aid."
"We are not the Foe, Joe."

On cue from the conductor,
The percussion section struck
And an octave of innocence
Was cracked by the cymbal
Of bullet on bone,
Bone on bone
Broken notes heaped in a crescendo of shame;

A stanza of strangers
Who measured their lives
In a cup of land
Lay like slaughtered sheep
In a yellow sleep;

   In the Village of Song My
   Walked G.I. Joe
   Searching for the Foe
   Looking for the Foe, Joe.

Part Three

$\mathcal{M}$OST AMERICANS look back upon the impeachment proceedings of 1974 as one of those moments in our history when men and women of conscience and conviction rose up and struck a blow for the preservation of our Constitution and the rule of law. Memory has a way of enlarging events, of simplifying and editing them to suit our best recollection of ourselves.

The palpable fear of the unknown consequences that might follow from stamping the red letter of impeachment on the brow of a President; the spasms in our national nervous system; the partisan division within the House Judiciary Committee and across the country; the volatility of international tensions—all have been airbrushed by time into a gray oblivion. There remains in the mind's eye only the color-chromatic portrait of demigods and demagogues, heroes and heretics, depending upon one's politics or perceptions.

Bookshelves are now bursting with volumes that analyze the corrosive effects of Watergate, the events which led to the unmaking of the President, or how nice guys sometimes finish first. Scholars and political sages, however, have had to peer into this extraordinary period of time through a window often rendered opaque by partisan caucuses, closed sessions and public poses that blurred or shaded into obscurity the nuances, the subtle shift of events and the quiet alliances that culminated in the forced resignation of a President.

Perhaps each of us will one day disclose how we reached our separate versions of the truth; what it was like, particularly for Republicans, to walk the tightrope between disloyalty to party and disloyalty to principle, between the dictates of conscience and the demands of con-

45

stituents; and what effect the entire experience had on each of us as individuals.

I shall never forget how bone-weary the nation had become from the repetition of the word "Watergate." Once, in the summer of 1973, when I was on a four-hundred-mile walk through the coastal area of my district, I spoke at a fund-raising dinner held in my behalf. At the conclusion of the dinner one of my supporters got up and said, "When's this Watergate thing going to end?"

My response was, "Not for a long time and it shouldn't. We should not tolerate the type of abuses that have occurred and until all of the facts come out, the Senate Committee should continue."

My questioner countered, "But they didn't do anything different than everybody else except they used electronic spies."

I agreed but pointed out, "I doubt whether it was done on such a systematic basis but even assuming that it was, the fact that abuses have occurred in the past does not justify our allowing them to continue in the future."

It was not the response that most of those in attendance that evening had paid to hear. It left the bitter taste of disappointment on their tongues as they got up from their tables.

I didn't sleep well that night. I could see the antagonism that was developing among the people, a good deal of it directed toward me for failing to support President Nixon's plea to stanch the flow of blood from this self-inflicted wound.

The next day, during the course of a twenty-two-mile hike, I left the road to find relief from the sun and heat. What was to be a short pause lengthened into minutes.

I was overwhelmed by the peace of the woods, the scent of the pines, the serenity of the trees.

The pressure of maintaining my walk schedule shattered the pleasure of the experience. That night, I tried to retrieve the mystical sensation of that brief interlude with nature—its splendor and perfection, so uncluttered by the complexities and connivances of man.

A Little Greener Now

I feel a little greener,
cleaner somehow for
having walked through
the woods today.

The wind whispered to the
trees in hushed tones,
though not fully heard,
could still be understood.

Pines pierced the sky
and held back the light
from the night beneath,
where minor creatures went at ease,
and rocks wore moss
in cool shades of suede.

Silence there was shattered
only by a caw or winged cry,
some sudden dark flutter
that warned all others of
the strange passerby.

I paused just long enough
under those needled boughs
to hear a harmony too perfect
to be reproduced by man.

I hugged the shadows, kissed the leaves,
was loved in return, it seemed,
by the breeze,
and felt the green fill of life
flow from the trees
gently into me.

Then I turned and left
that dark unmapped retreat
and dissolved into the
roar and ruin of the street.

The Gates of Hays

The foul breath of scandal
hangs heavy from
the high ceilings
of Congress now.

Some are sent scrambling
to pull up the drawbridges
of their own sins;
others rally 'round
their fallen friend
to dress, in their tortured fashion,
his wounds with words
of their compassion.

Rancor and recriminations
become items on the daily agenda
as the Nation's drumbeat
of outrage
and assault begins.

"Resign, Mr. Chairman, before
the putrid smell
infects all in this chamber
as well."

"He's innocent until guilt's
confirmed," comes the retort.

It's the sort of poison
we thought was drained
from our system
just a season or so
ago.

One can witness,
in this historic hall,
the pious and petrified
and those who rush
to teletype to all
the moral pocks and peccadillos
of public men. . . .

The Magna Carta arrives today
from across the sea,
sacred testament of the
birth of liberty.

While Congress contemplates
whether a jealous mistress
is, indeed, the law.

Part Four

$\mathcal{M}$Y COLLEGE roommate, Charles Wing, is quite simply a genius—author, oceanographer, physicist, artist, musician, mechanic and carpenter. In short, he is that man for all seasons.

In spite of his complexity—rather, because of it—he is essentially a simple man who takes great delight in simple pleasures. He usually wears a faded flannel shirt, old jeans, lace-up boots and wire-rimmed glasses and can be found on many mornings over the kitchen stove making blueberry muffins and home fries.

It came as no surprise to us when he abandoned his teaching position at MIT to return with his family to Maine to live on an old farm. There, amid his pigs, chickens and vegetable gardens, he could sink his roots deep into the rocky soil that remains a symbol of Yankee spirit and independence. Charlie and his wife, Susan, are the founders of Cornerstones, a school they operate in Brunswick, Maine, teaching people how to construct affordable new homes or to retrofit older ones, maximizing nature's gifts in a post-industrial age of dwindling fossil fuels.

"Wings on Woolwich" was written during our first visit to Charlie and Susan's farm in Woolwich, Maine.

Wings on Woolwich

Come visit our new old farm
and bring the children
to enjoy the charm
of rolling down
the color and curve
of camel hills
free from hurt
away from harm.

Come sit beneath the limb
of our aging oak
and listen to the leaves
quietly soak
in the current of
warm wind.

Come see the shack
filled with fifty baby chicks,
a pen stocked with the
pink grunt of a pig
and the garden sprung
with ears of corn
and pods of peas.

Come now to our no-horse farm
where the fields are reamed
by an iron-lunged machine
who drinks from a trough
filled with yellow gasoline.

Come meet our strange neighbors
who will quietly auto
into our yard to talk
and then wait patiently
for us to knock
upon their door.

Come help us mend
the splintered legs
of a decaying barn
that prompts on sight
the faint alarm
of pending loss.

Come soon,
and bring with you
a flask of Falernian,
oh, even Gallo wine,
so we can drink and dine
while man seeks
and soils the moon.

Come sit with us
under the night,
and play crosswords
with the stars;
come taste the flavor
of our farm
and touch the hand
of friendship.

Part Five

cMy wife, Diane, is hard to capture in print. She is the most fascinating person that I know. From a distance she appears to be only a beautiful woman. Up close, she has as many facets as a diamond.

She is a cultivator of flowers, a friend of children, the daughter of older folks, an attraction to men and yet not a threat to women. She is fiercely independent, a feminist who is quintessentially feminine. She possesses an inner strength and genuine love for all things that literally glows in her face. It is a magnetic force that draws the very best from the people that she meets.

Whenever I write about Diane, I associate her with gardens and groves—their complexity, quiet strength and serenity, the green pulse of life itself.

The tree is a great symbol to me. It is life, knowledge, growth. It is whipped by the winds as we are by emotions. It knows moments of brilliance and barrenness. It bends under the weight and stress of the elements. Sometimes it is scarred by thoughtless people.

But if its roots are well planted in the soil, with determination and luck, it will broaden over the years and stand in tall serenity, facing the seasons with an assurance and calm acceptance of the order of the universe.

So it has been with Diane—my wife, my lover, my friend.

The Grove

Come and touch me now, Diana,
And let your boughs
Brush against my face.

Entwine
Your shadow into mine
While our limbs are still green
And the white of winter
Is a season or two away;

The sun is high
Our roots dig deep
And songs still leap among our leaves;

But today the forest's springs seem quieter
And yesterday the squirrels were hiding
Chestnuts in some hollowed trees.

An Untitled Poem About

Diane,
a quiet bubble of life
seeping through neglected soils,
reversing the rooted,
spreading seeds, pulling weeds,
and turning brown to green.

Somehow you pushed through
the concrete that surrounds
my soul,
and with your gentle flow
washed a mind of war and passion
with the secrets of the sea.

If I seem too silent at times,
it's that I'm listening to
the flower you planted
crawling up my spine.

I love you.

Quiet Leaves

It rests there,
just beneath the
shadow of our lives.

An invisible cord
lying mostly loose and limp,
like a rope temporarily
abandoned by a child.

Remember? Eight years ago,
and a summer for measure,
we looped it around our waist,
shook a fist at the sky,
and dared the elements
to fray our faith.

In the instant of an emotion
it has snapped taut and tense,
and sometimes even chafed
our skin
until the liquid within
seeped into vision
and ran vocal.

And those few quiet creatures
who sought the comfort of our shade,
ceased their song and clung
to our swaying limbs,
as our leaves rustled
in the shifting winds.

But it held,
and now hangs loose again.
And we are one,
standing in the calm
of an unalterable
love.

Summer Still

In a beach house
last July,
we sat on the edge
of the sea
facing roaring breakers
amplified then by
night.

Our sons, fed and slapped
with happy sunburns,
were tucked in quilted sleep
and the radio sang of
Christ the Superstar.

The reading lamp
in the wide window
served as a beacon
to strange night travelers,
creatures the daylight
somehow hides,
and large white moths,
flying leucocytes of sorts,
beat their wings in agony
against the tempered
glass.

I am sitting there even now
as September dries the salt
and suntan oil from our smiles.
The sea, the scent, the sound
is still fresh,
and that instant when
I looked up and caught
your eyes fixed on mine,
I felt love leap and flash,
the quick glint of sun on a silver fish,
and then returned to read
a book of poems.

Voices

I hear a voice inside
the voice that others hear
which sounds to me
much as it did yesterday
and the year before.

It whispers about the days
when we lay browned
upon the beaches
of distant towns
and read the lips
of white sighs
hanging in the sky.

We skipped our laughter
into the sea
and made love
in a castle of sand
wearing the salt
as our wedding band,
and just for fun
we had seagulls and sailboats
for dinner,
roasted by the sun.

But somehow clouds always
have to blow away,
just as rivers change
from day to day
and the dawn chases
morning dew over
meadows.

Yes, Time has a mind
to run away
like a butterfly who
stops one day
to touch you
with its grace
and then leaves
to kiss the flower
of another face.

Still, when I look
into your eyes
I can see the light
that showed my shadow
how to smile
and made the night
as bright
as noon.

One day,
you'll catch a cloud
and float away
while I pour
an afternoon tea.

But I'll find you somewhere
just beyond the sea,
on the other side of
eternity.

Part Six

You did not hear them coming. You hardly heard
them go. The grass bent down, sprang up again.
They passed like cloud shadows downhill . . . the
boys of summer, running.
—RAY BRADBURY, *Dandelion Wine*

DURING THEIR early years, I used to write poems for my sons, usually on their birthdays. I am among those sentimental, over-indulgent, too-proud parents who look into the eyes of their children and see their innocence, their idealism, their promise. I am one who hopes that they will not be stained by pettiness or vulgarity or narrow-minded ambition during their years; that life will always be vivid, bold and bright.

Even amid the joy of those moments that I share with them, my ears are filled with the loud tick of Time, the whispery scratch of sand sliding through the neck of an hourglass. And I try desperately to freeze Time, with a camera, a pose, a poem, before they run off and roll down the hills of their futures.

Christopher Sunshine

Tonight, when I looked
at my son's small, empty shoes
lying scattered on the floor,
I saw, for just a moment,
the fears and friends
that fill his day.

I stepped into his room
to listen to the
soft sound of his dreams,
to kiss his head, ask him to stay,
so that the hearth would always
smell of burnt marshmallow puffs
and the snowman would not lose
his charcoal smile
in the warm wind
of another Spring.

But the sundial had been set
and I could see the shadow
on his face
sweeping by the minutes
of ice cream and innocence.

As I stood there in the darkness
I remembered my father's shoes
at the foot of my childhood stairs,
and I wondered then—and now—

When will you leave me?

To Kevin, on Your Birthday

Who would believe that the
liquids of love once met
And fashioned your being into
a knot intrinsicate?

That six times you've circled the sun since
you pushed through that fold in nature's purse
And cried to white-smocked shepherds
to increase the rolls of the universe?

But a moment ago you were—yes—
bald, colicky and distressingly unsteady,
And suddenly you stand before me,
tall, tawny and elastically athletic.

From white seed to green sapling,
from idle chatter to innocent conversation,
And wide-eyed vacancy
to psychedelic imagination;

I watch your eyes bounce over
the mad-hatter rhymes of Dr. Seuss
And think of dewdrops swelling
on the boughs of a slender spruce;

And when you spring forward
to lash a ball or sail a kite,
I hear a brook running in the forest,
and see a bird fixed in the web of sunlight;

How long does it take a falling star
to scratch its light on the blackboard of night?
Longer than for you to laugh at this
beautiful metamorphosis.

Reflections

Lingering in the loneliness of a chairless room,
I watched a cluster of birch trees
sway their naked limbs
to the quiet strings
of a chordless breeze.

The white light of morning,
splintered by their bony fingers,
blew arterial shadows across my wall,
as it kissed the earth outside
washed by an early rainfall.

But the silence of a Sunday was broken
by the flower faces of my children,
as their laughter bubbled ahead of their legs
    into my lap,
pushing, teasing, rolling,
around my neck,
    down my back.

OFF, you cubs, OUT.
I want to wander down the corridors of my memory.
Wait—don't go. Tomorrow you'll fly free,
I know that little boys leave Puff in Hanilee.

Just leave me the magic of your shingled hair
hanging over an incautious ear,
sticky cotton-candy kisses,
water-colored scare-crowed men,
and sad clowns with finger painted frowns.

When I cannot hear the springtide in your voices
and see the Tinkertoy secrets in your eyes,
there will be time enough to look at birch trees and shadows
    on a Sunday morning.

Part Seven

cAFTER THE vote on Article I of the resolution to impeach Richard Nixon, I returned to Maine to explain to the people of my state the reasons for my vote. When I returned to Washington to continue the debate on the resolution, one of my colleagues told me that he wanted to explain his vote to his constituents but was having some difficulty in drafting a statement.

I offered to let him use as a guide the speech I had just made. He, apparently, found it suitable for his needs since he simply deleted the references to Maine and substituted the name of his own state. Several days later, I saw portions of my speech reprinted on the editorial page of one of the nation's largest papers, now attributed to its new author. The article prompted me to jot down a light-hearted note to myself, rationalizing dubiously that a speech delivered, or a song sung, by anyone but its author must necessarily be inferior.

The Plagiarist

Someone stole my song
last night and sang it
out of tune.

So quick to steal my treasure,
he gathered up my words
without my measure
and stuffed them hurriedly
into his black bag.

And when he played
before the world
the melody soured
on the strings
and notes fell from
the chords on ears
in agony.

To you who would
beggar me of my songs
and pretend to all
that you are their creator:
Take care. When you take
my words, you also
steal my measure.

Part Eight

ONE OF the most difficult assignments I had during my first year at Bowdoin College was to write a sonnet for an English course. My principal occupation at that time was playing guard on the college basketball team. Not only did poetry strike me at that time as particularly inappropriate for a macho-minded basketball player, but I also felt uniquely ill-equipped to write it.

One day while cramming for a biology exam in the library, I came across a medical study that had been conducted to try to establish a connection between weather conditions and the mating instinct among animals. It occurred to me that the notion that the weather vane could alter love among humans should be my first poem.

Can Season Be the Reason?

Winter freezes summer blood to ice,
And chills the passions that await the spring;
The lover suffers seasoned sacrifice,
At Altars bleak with crystal covering.

What heart can hold a love in winter's time,
When even Nature slacks her passioned pace,
When minor creatures flee the upper clime,
For warmer realms of borrowed, burrowed space?

But spring has courage to oppose the cold,
And passes on to those in love the same;
The sounds of life and future birth take hold,
Of human ears that closed at winter's name.

Yet is it fair to unimpassioned reason
To say that love depends upon a season?

October Sunday

Autumn just touches you
one day,
in a way that
no other moment
does.

Trees surrender their green
for gold
at the first touch of cold
and cry quietly
in color
at the betrayal of the
sun.

The wind paints flesh
the hue of apple skins,
spirits soar in concrete stadiums,
while winter's scout
cuts the throats of perennials
and muffles the pain in
ice.

Strange, how we rejoice
at the brilliance of
the red,
knowing their lives
are nearly dead,
and our children play
in paper graves
dug by fallen
leaves.

Stranger still, the custom
of mourning the death
of summer
with a family ride
through the countryside
pointing at the splendor of it
all.

Popham Beach

Here at Popham,
everything is original,
lyrical in beauty.

A shelf of wild grass
drops off
to a horseshoe mile
of warm sensuous sand
pounded endlessly
by the white tail
of that frantic
beast we call Atlantic.

A songburst of sun
bounces off the
soft edges of powdered glass
until the eye is relieved
by a crow's nest peer
of the vagrant wisps
of cotton clouds
spun from some unseen
circus machine.

And poised on a string
of hunger hangs
a mackerel gull
until from high he spies
a silver shimmer
and then drops dead
into the curl of a wave,
emerging in flight and proud,
his bill filled with a
fisheye of survival.

Yes, everything here is natural . . .
except, that is, the cottages,
and a boulder-braced trailer park,
that breaks the beauty of the sea.

Look: over there is a man
falling drunk in the sun,
sprawling in the sand like
an aging up-ended crab
or a white-whiskered dog
wounded by a hit and run.

Oh, school of sandpipers,
rustling about like legged leaves,
had you the weight and will
to carry him away
on this sabbath day
and free the beach of man
and his malady.

Diamond Head

When dusk dissolves
in the East,
the sun hangs high
on Diamond Head,
bleaching beaches into white,
and turning flesh red
beyond relief;

Hawaii is an island of Eden
lush with plants and
the ganglia of banyan trees,
whose roots reverse their course
from limbs to add new
stanchions of stability.

Warm trade winds that filled
the sails of merchant ships
still blow and bend
the trees to bows,
and dark-skinned children
with smiles of coconut
greet the surf
on waxed petals
struck from wood.

There is a permanence here
despite the passing of other ages,
but no relief comes to this constancy,
no shift occurs between the seasons.

This isle of bright
and green glory
sees no spring rites
feels no soft surge
when ice breaks
oozing liquid from within,
when water fills the ruts
cut by winter's knife
and sends them running
into brooks.

There is no autumn
to mark the burnished
death of one more year,
no herald of the cold to come,
no crystal flakes gather here
to pave the path for swishing skates.

Summer sings forever here,
proud, perpetual and solitary.
Even the light rain
if sent, perchance, in adversity
arrives in quiet harmony.

One could grow old in Hawaii
just gazing into the green sea,
and but for the annular rings
sewn on the trunks of palm trees,
never know what age he was
or that in which he lived.

Coastal Zones

I've often wondered
what territorial prerogatives
mark the Maine coastal waters,
I mean, what lines are drawn
by lobstermen dumping and hauling pots,
circling 'round their salted buoys
with motors chugging soft?

Maybe it's done
without any formal thought,
just a knowing nod,
a mute acknowledgment
"This is mine, that's yourn."

Perhaps that's line enough.

Spring Metaphor

April is here again
and brings a season
in search of some
metaphor.

Summer, for me, leans lazily,
a garden rake
against a weathered
door.

Autumn is a splendored messenger
that mounts, then rides
its horse to death.

And Winter touches
skin and bones,
with a country doctor's
cold compress.

But you, Spring,
you come bugling
through morning glories,
shouting for all
to come and see.

You come skipping
down the street,
a child wearing
a brand new suit
without a hint
of modesty.

The Promise
For Pete and Judi Dawkins

Spring came late
this year,
or, perhaps, it's just
that Winter refused
to leave.

The sky was gray
and cold so long
that April came
with snow instead
of rain.

Pine trees and evergreens
were blown brown,
birch trees lay
bowed to the ground
in unwilling homage
to the crown of white
that reigns in the kingdom
of snow and ice.

But just the other day
about the first of May
there appeared the sun
like some burning salmon
on a run.

Suddenly brilliant flower heads
emerged in painless birth,
rows of rainbows spread,
petals spun in silken thread.

Trees began to shout in green
while the season's
feathered supplicants
leapt among their leaves,
and children could be seen
skipping rope, in
new and tattered jeans.

Motion was everywhere, in everything,
even the night began to sing
with crickets' busy legs;
proud robins and jays sent trills
through valved lutes and piccolos
hidden safely in their
happy throats.

Swollen ridges and ruts
sagged as the liquid beneath
rose and ran rippling
into the streets;
dogs bounced and barked
and galloped through
the city parks.

Sunshine, shadows
sounds and echoes were abound,
song was in the air and
color in riot everywhere.

One transparent moment in May
I saw the promise of rebirth,
heard the whisper of repair.

Flight to Phoenix

I soar now,
a hawk with flaming eyes,
high above canyons and groves,
cleaving through the clouds.

Alone, at last,
except for the whisper
of the wind.

Here I hover, feather,
without hood or chain,
caught in no man's cage
suffering no imprisoned rage.

A thought flits below,
stirring leaves and branches
ever so . . . as I
rush, wings tucked,
to pluck it screaming
from the brush
and fill my hungry
wit.

Part Nine

IN SEPTEMBER of 1976, I was campaigning for re-election in northern Maine. One of my district representatives and I had just finished attending a chicken barbecue in the town of Sinclair. As we started the long drive back through the heavily wooded area, I saw something move in the brush off to my right. I yelled "stop" and I remember reflexively slamming my right foot to the floor of my passenger's seat.

Suddenly a large doe burst across the highway and cleared the span of the road in two bounds. Seconds later a small fawn struggled out of a trench on thin legs, and the right side of our car smashed into it.

Writing is a cathartic experience for me, a blood-letting of sorts. When a thought enters my mind, it preoccupies every waking moment until I purge it on paper. So it was with the death of the fawn. It poisoned my entire system until I could drain the horror of that moment away with my pen.

The Wound

Forgive me, for I know
What I have done.
I've taken a child
Of the woods
In the gunsight
Of my hood.

Metal and chrome
Sheared sinew from bone
And blasted blood
Through thin veins
Into a tiny brain.

A sudden and sickening crack!
A cry not heard.
STOP. Go back.
Hit it again.
No. Just STOP!

A half-look back in primal terror.
The fawn wriggling on her back
Her legs kicking in the air
Struggling to correct the error
Of her Executioner.

How do I comfort the dying?
Hold my hand over
The heart beating hot,
Sighing, "Be still, lie softly—
It's all right,"
Knowing it's not?

Panic and now the calm,
The wagging tail slowing,
Life draining away
Into some invisible pool,
The spirit now unredeemable.

The open eye
Staring into the sky,
Looking for yet another sun
To do the things
Tomorrow has left undone,
Until it hardens
Cold and calm
As glass.

Mother in the tall grass,
You failed to read the sign—
It was marked in blacktop,
The whine of wheels
Warned you to stop.

Why did you spring
Across the road just then
And drop your baby into
The breech of chance
At odds with all circumstance?

No purpose is served
In begging the question.

Mother in the woods:
STOP staring.
Stop waiting.
Your child's not coming.
Her tail's stopped wagging.

Let me linger here
Amid the tumid ruins
Of my after thoughts
Alone with the horror
That I have wrought.

Part Ten

During a visit to my hometown of Bangor in the fall of 1974, I stopped to say hello to some of the patients at the city's hospital.

I was told that an old friend of mine would like to see me. When I walked into his room, the excitement and anticipation of seeing him was shattered by a sledgehammer of shock.

The man who was once the big, burly, blue-eyed, red-cheeked Irish police chief, who was such a symbol of strength and vigor, who spent so many years coaching young boys' athletic teams in his off-duty hours, now lay withered, helpless and unrecognizable.

He looked at me and said, "Oh, Billy, look at what's happened to me." And then he started to cry.

I just held his hand and didn't try to stop the tears that seemed to well up from deep within my throat. He died two days later.

Apparition

Today, I saw the apparition of a friend,
a former tutor, as he lay in fear,
drained and shriveled
in a white hospital bier.

In his bleeding eyes could be seen
a painful whimpering notion
that his intrinsic knot,
of tissue and thought
of muscle and motion,
had started to rot.
Yes, he knew he was
at last falling apart.

Now, I have witnessed death before—
travelers strewn about on highways
like so much litter,
babies beaten blue by
parents who were bitter,
and the suicide's solitary drop
from bridges of despair—
none left life in silence,
all were bruised and swollen,
pounded by some visible violence.

But I never saw death
come silently from inside
to steal a man's honor
and body and pride.
No, I never saw
a man's vital cords
cut and quartered by
a million tiny swords.

Who is the captain of this horde,
this hellish hidden army
that assaults man, unchecked by conscience
or articles of morality?
What glory can there be
in waging this cellular war?
What gain in claiming the
marrow of this man's core?

The questions, of course, died unanswered.
The angry cells just multiplied with abandon
and sundered sinew into gauze
until their victim picked
no doubt at random
signed away to pneumonia
or some secondary cause.

For the first time, I heard
the count and cadence of cancer.
It was slow, drip, drip,
and I witnessed the fiber
of a part of my past
melting like the wax
of a sallow candle.

Part Eleven

IN THE summer of 1971, Diane and I learned that John Carradine was coming to the University of Maine to give dramatic readings. We were eager to attend, to see an actor of his stature.

Moments before the performance was scheduled to begin, Hauck Auditorium was cast into total darkness. A voice boomed out through the amplification system, quoting from the Book of Genesis. It was so deep and sonorous it could have been the voice of God. Suddenly, a spotlight illuminated the source of our momentary terror. One could feel the surprise that swept through the audience.

John Carradine stood near the center of the stage, dressed in a dark suit that had been cleaned and pressed too many times, that now hung too large on his gaunt frame. His hair was long and shaggy, giving his thin face a sad, hounddog appearance. What struck me most at that moment, however, was that his body seemed to be undergoing some painful transformation. His arthritic hands were swollen and twisted. His shoes seemed much larger than his feet. I concluded that they served to accommodate toes that were gnarled and inverted.

As he spoke, his feet were planted in one spot, as if they had taken root while his whole body swayed back and forth to the rhythm of his words. It occurred to me that, like a number of heroes in Greek mythology, Carradine in the hour of his impending death would metamorphose into another form of life. In his case a cypress tree seemed appropriate.

113

We soon became oblivious to his appearance, however. His voice simply overpowered our eyes. For more than two hours that evening, we sat in silence, soldered by his voice to the thoughts of our greatest poets and philosophers.

The Actor

We sat in dry silence
one midsummer night
waiting for the evening's
guest to appear,
when, through our senses
a voice suddenly was thrown;
amplified by the darkness,
it liquefied our bones.

Black thunderclouds cracked
and boomed their terror
through the canyons
of our inner thoughts.

But a flood of light then
spilled across the stage
and exposed the lie
that the house that
held this voice
was equally sublime.

Wounded whispers of surprise
fled through the garden
of felt seats;
lisping leaves touched
by an evening breeze
rivulets of rain seeping
through a gravel lane.

The actor's face, pole-thin,
was draped on the hanger
of his frame;
flesh lantern, oracles for eyes,
his sorrow and fame
ran like a bleeding vein.

His fingers tortured by time
clung like some leafless vine
at the hollow of his belt
except to raise an essential note;
his shoes were worn intentionally large
as if to permit his twisted toes to invert
in their mad search
for some unseen stream.

This head that once celebrated
its noonday in the sun
and ran the wind through its hair,
stood there,
decaying, pigment fading
into pain.

But the voice,
sovereign, and savage,
swallowed its dwindling shell,
held history and poetry
on each chord
and burned them in sulphur
and a flame of words.

Astral Thought

Man stands tense
to step among the stars,
his jargon brimmed with
non-declining quasars
and soon we're told
he'll tell us whether
life exists on Mars.

The thought of screaming
through the night
laminated to a ray
of light
is heavy seed indeed.

But if the choice
were mine to make,
knowing life to be at stake,
I would choose to know
the secret of the oak
standing in tall serenity,
asking not of origin,
caring not for destiny,
satisfied, it seems, to be.

Part Twelve

Dɪᴀɴᴇ ᴀɴᴅ I have been intensely conscious and critical of the commercialism of Christmas for many years. The holiday (holy day) has been sprinkled by so much tinsel, artificial snow and plastic decoration that the original purpose of celebrating the birth of Christ has been all but buried by the army of Tinkertoy trucks that graces every tree and television set.

We have tried to stress the spiritual significance of the day and season to our sons and to minimize the materialism that is so pervasive. We have not been entirely successful in that effort. Usually, we end up victims of the hysteria that sweeps across the country, buying last-minute gifts for family members or friends who have showered us with evidence of their love and affection, thereby forcing us to go surging into the waves of humanity that flood the cash-out counters of the shopping centers that have spread across the landscape of this country.

On Christmas Eve 1971, thoroughly exhausted, we were settled in front of the fireplace of our home, listening to records, when we received a phone call from a friend who asked if we would be willing to take care of a young child whose mother had been taken to a hospital that day.

Although we quickly agreed, I remained uneasy about how to comfort a young boy whose poverty now included the loss of his mother's love and companionship on this special night.

Christmas Eve

Christmas eve, 1971,
we feel neither joy
nor sorrow, only a
quiet sort of love.

The night outside
is wet with rain,
the room filled
with the strains
of folk and soul
and a melting satisfaction
as we await the
coming of the dawn.

Huddled here in this home
of wood and stone
we watch the coals burn gray
then disintegrate.
Our children regenerate
in dreams of stockings
filled with candy, toys
and fat figments of
bearded joy.

Who is this stranger
that came to share tonight,
this man-child orphaned
on the eve of birth?

Will tomorrow bring
his mother back to health
and shake him awake
from the nightmare of loss?

Take this bed, child,
morning will break,
tomorrow will speak,
but tonight,
rub your wounds
with the salve
of sleep.

Part Thirteen

Part Fifteen

BETWEEN 1969 and 1971, I served as a prosecuting attorney in the Penobscot County Attorney's Office. Part of my responsibility was the investigation of highway traffic deaths as well as homicides and suicides. My first investigation was a memorable one. I was having dinner with my family when the phone rang and I was asked to proceed to the scene of a highway fatality. I recall the fear that struck me. I didn't want to go.

Upon arrival, I saw the bodies of an old man and his grandson. They had been on their way to a fishing trip when the grandfather lost control of the car.

Death is an abstraction for most of us. We read about it in the papers daily, we see it in magazines or simulated in movies or on television. Even when it touches us, we usually face it under the mitigating circumstances of a church service, the cosmetic embellishments of the funeral director, flowers, hymnals and the veil of quiet tears.

Most of us are spared the brutality of witnessing violent death and the degradation of the body which houses our souls. It is an innocence that, once lost, can never be regained.

I recall being upset not only with the grisly scene but at the seeming indifference of the investigators. I failed to realize at the time that indifference or callousness may be the only way for those who must confront death each day to preserve their sanity.

For the next two years, I saw too many deaths and autopsies. I could never write about them again. I was relieved when my term of office ended.

Death on 95

The muted ring of the telephone
Spilled into the wine of my after-dinner thoughts:
"Accident on Route 95—two fatalities
Proceed to the scene—would you please."

The eggshell of evening was closing
On the center of the sun
And in the distance the strobic blue lights
Leapt across the highway,
Yelling of tragedy.

Over a guardrail and down the bank
A car rested on its side,
The body dismembered, contents disgorged,
A soiled bag of garbage
Scattered on the roadside from a fleeting window.

An old man lay stretched in the straw
Twisted like licorice
His jaws sprung open by the horror of the instant,
As if he died with a scream
Locked in his throat;
An angry god must have wrenched
His soul from his bowels, I thought,
And flung it, a piece of suet,
To the watchdog of hell.

Nearby a younger man
Was bent in a fetal clump,
His face painted a purposeless plaid
By the mad artist of the accident.

The morticians were quick and sure
In loading the litter,
Pausing only to ask for names
And next of kin,
Unaware that the sight of two plastic sacks
Speeding off in their polished Cadillac
Somehow seemed obscene.

Then only the State Police remained
With cardboard faces,
Expressionless, one shaking his head,
"Lost 'er on the curve, I guess."

Two strangers from a distant state
Had woven their years into unrehearsed patterns
Which were unraveled in a moment
Of crushed metal and glass—

But there were no wet eyes on Route 95.

That night while shadows from the street
Slipped across the ceiling of my room
I squeezed the sounds of my wife and children
    sleeping,
Into my hands and wept.

Epitaph

Here lies a man
who died in youth
for no apparent cause.

A post mortem chart
said a question mark
was wrapped around
his heart.

Part Fourteen

Between the idea
And the reality
Between the motion
And the act
Falls the Shadow.
　　—T. S. ELIOT, "The Hollow Men"

IN THE late summer of 1976, I came across a brief article in *The New York Times* that described the stabbing death of a young man in Greenwich Village. The senseless slaughter of innocent people no longer seems to cause enduring shock to those who inhabit or endure life in our urban centers. The victim is, for the most part, anonymous. There is no connection to the agony and grief of the surviving relatives. The news may dominate the day's conversation but then is lost in the stream of escalating food prices, rising unemployment statistics or the threat of a public service strike. Today, the living do not pause long for those who are tallied among the lost.

What separated this particular tragedy from the steady flow of savagery that has somehow been accommodated in our daily lives was the irony of this man's death. He had been asked by a friend to come to Greenwich Village and help move furniture into another apartment. He initially declined to do so because of his fear of the violence in the neighborhood and because he had to attend a birthday party for his father. Friendship prevailed and he finally relented. His greatest fear became a violent reality.

Terror in the Village

Danger swelled up
and took form
in the darkness,
a dagger poised
for some stranger
who challenged its point.

One came who feared
the night and the streets
filled with broken veins
that knew the pain
that needles track.

But came in love
for a friend,
when suddenly a shadow
moved in his path.

Theft, caught in the act,
recoiled in violence,
plunged its steel
into the stranger's heart
that pumped life out
through arteries shredded apart.

A young man fled
down Bleecker Street.
"Hispanic," they said.

Father, come take your son,
whose heart was
filled with fear
and love.

Epilogue

When the night finally comes
and wraps us in darkness
with its shawl,

and our eyes are sutured
shut by the mortician's cold
needlepoint;

when our children are old
and those who are now
but seed in young boys' loins
strut in arrogance and sweet lust;

let no one trample upon our trust
tipping the tablets that
mark our bones
or scrawl obscenities
in colored chalk.

No, let those who then live
come in silence
and know that
in our grove,
beneath our stones
lie two who laughed and sang
knowing time could not be slowed
or common doom delayed.

And so spent it all
locked in love with everything.

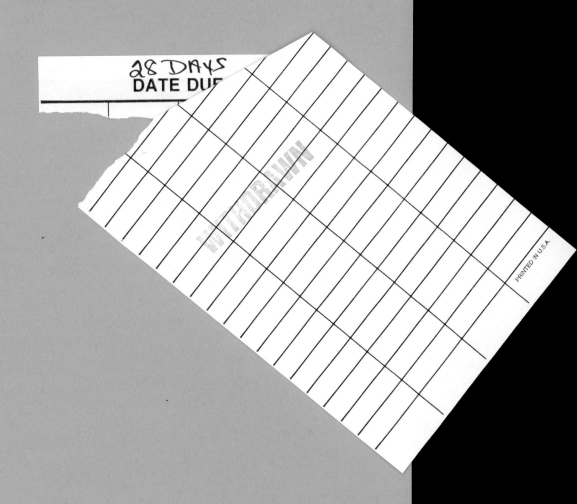

28 DAYS
DATE DUE

PRINTED IN U.S.A.